I0560511

RISING
FROM
THE FIRE

ALSO BY THE AUTHOR

RESTORED TO WHOLENESS

SURRENDERING TO WHO YOU ARE

FREE YOUR SOUL

THE LOVE WITHIN

THE HARMONY WITHIN

THE WISDOM WITHIN

THE HOME WITHIN

LIFE ON FIRE JOURNAL

Please scan the link above to view
all the titles currently available by
this author. Thank you.

RISING FROM THE FIRE

Inspirational Reflections on Healing, Resilience, and Burning Brighter

MURIEL OKUBO

DOCTOR OF ASIAN MEDICINE

Copyright @ 2025 by Muriel Okubo
Written and designed by Muriel Okubo
All Rights Reserved.

No part of this book may be reproduced, distributed, transmitted or amended in any form or by any means, including photocopying, recording, or other electronic or mechanical methods, without prior written permission of the publisher, except in the case of brief quotations embodied in reviews and specific other noncommercial uses permitted by copyright law. No graphics or images from this book may be copied or retransmitted without the Muriel Okubo's express written permission.

Ebook ISBN: 978-1-998695-07-2
PB ISBN: 978-1-998695-05-8
HC ISBN: 978-1-998695-06-5

To everyone on this journey of life,
choosing light over the dark.

Dear Friend,

You're the alchemist of your life. Within you, indwells a divine power to change all your hardships into goodness and greatness. No darkness can defeat your light. You can choose love, peace, harmony, health, joy, and success in every moment.

Whatever it is that you're desiring, make the choice to set yourself up for success intentionally. Crowd out your thoughts that tell you you can't make it or it's impossible. You were created as a being of love and light —there is nowhere you can't go or achieve.

Fill yourself with love, light, truth, possibility, and all you desire and let it radiate back to you. This is how you turn the darkness into light...every single day.

You got this, my friend.

TABLE OF CONTENTS

INTRODUCTION

We each face hardships—unique fires of all sizes that test our resilience. They challenge us deeply, urging us to fight for our lives. Hardships come in many forms: the death of a loved one, a serious illness, the breakdown of a relationship, a natural disaster, or a profound trauma—anything that forces us into survival mode. We'll recognize our fire because it will be unforgettable, life-changing, and push us beyond our limits.

If you've endured these fires, you understand the divine strength and perseverance it takes to overcome them. Being here means you're a survivor—an overcomer. I honour your resilience.

You are not alone, and these messages are for you.

Let the fire that nearly consumed you be the force that ignites the greatness within. Through tragedy and chaos, you have been reborn, repurposing your life with newfound strength. The energy you've gained fuels your journey back to purpose. Suddenly, the adages about transformation resonate more deeply than ever before:

Like a phoenix, you rise from the ashes.
The strongest steel is forged in the hottest fire.
What doesn't kill you makes you stronger.
You are fire—burning with purpose.
When faced with flames, fight fire with fire.

These sayings exist for a reason. In the face of turmoil and chaos, you'll draw a surge of survival energy from the deepest part of yourself. When you've survived the unimaginable, meaning will emerge from the rubble and ash, guiding you forward. These verses hold your story of your resilience—of how you will paint the world with your radiant light. A part of you was lost in the fire, but you're here to rise from it and live anew.

In these verses, I remind you that what you overcame during such trials is never easy. As a witness and survivor, I understand the power of what fire can do—it can consume or embolden, depending on your resolve. If you commit to keeping your light burning, it will guide you to victory. This journey is both exhausting and beautiful, demanding an extraordinary level of faith to persist when everything seems lost.

Let these verses speak to you in the way you need most—to comfort, heal, and strengthen you as you move forward. Their repetition is intentional, because healing requires reminding your heart and soul of the truth: who you are, what you've overcome, and why the world still needs you.

Let only the truth speak to you, offering what you need in the moments when understanding and connection matter most. Remember, healing is a process; be patient, compassionate, and kind to yourself along the way.

Every fire affects us differently, yet they all carry the same elements—survival, pain, faith, perseverance, challenge, resilience, and growth. Though each of us faces a unique fire, we stand together. United, we can help one another overcome.

Hold on to your light and never let it fade. The divine flicker within you—the force that carried you through —will continue to bless and illuminate every season of your life. Rebuild the world around you with the same beauty and brilliance that shines inside you.

As you move forward, safeguard your light, nurturing it with empowering thoughts and unwavering strength.

Never forget this divine force within you—one that the people in your life and the world still need. Your mission is far from over. Let your love overflow, fierce and unstoppable, like the lava flowing from a mountain.

Thank you for being here—you are seen, valued, and always supported.

*

Sometimes, the moments
that steal your breath away
are the moments
that force you to breathe again.
You might have endured a season like this.
Everything holds meaning in life—
the meaning you choose to give it.
Anything that has harmed you
can be transformed—
reshaped into something beautiful.
In devastation's aftermath
you are forced to seek life again.
Perspective shapes everything,
but only one view
grants you breath, beauty, life, and peace.

~your power to choose

*

I know with certainty
that every trial you've endured
was meant to test you,
to reveal how you would rise,
transforming pain
into something as beautiful as yourself.
You are emerging,
stepping out on the other side.
This test will not break you, my friend.
You will rise stronger,
wiser,
more compassionate,
more loving,
kinder to yourself,
and to all you meet.

~you're on your way

*

When you're ready,
take space for yourself.
Learn what gives you joy again,
what fills your soul with happiness.
Rediscover the thrill of life—
something new,
something true,
something meant just for you.
This is how you restore love,
filling in the spaces
that once were lost.

~come back to yourself

*

Let the hardship that almost decimated you
ignite your spirit with fire—
a passion for your purpose,
your mission,
your healing,
your future.
Let this flame spark your rebirth,
lifting you into a new vision
filled with radiance, love, joy,
peace, and gratitude.
You were resuscitated
to breathe life into the places
that need your presence and beauty.
Every moment is a choice—
a chance to animate the world
with the power only you hold.
Where is life calling you to rise?
What are you meant to breathe life into?

~sparking life

*

It's okay to feel tired,
to drift in uncertainty.
It's okay to long for the past
before the blaze
changed your world.
But you were never meant to stay
in the wilderness of pain.
Every day, you will rise
and create a new path.
This is your moment—
a chance to choose
a new adventure.
How boldly will you dream?
How far will you dare to go?

~creative path

*

This next step
is yours to take.
Some things will always be
beyond your control,
but others are within it.
Put your energy into what you can shape—
your response,
who you welcome into your life,
what you nourish yourself with,
the words you absorb,
the way your body moves,
the ideas you pursue,
the dreams you dare to imagine,
the places that call you.
Focus on the smallest things—
like your next breath.
Give yourself grace.
The world has shifted,
and you're writing a new story.

~focus your power

*

You don't need to have it figured out.
Listen to the quiet wisdom within—
it will stir ideas,
guide your steps,
show you where to go.
Trust the divine voice inside you—
it will carve a new path forward.
When your mind is still,
divine whispers will find you,
guiding you forward
toward blessings
beyond your imagination.
Nothing can replace what was lost,
nor is it meant to,
but love remains alive in your heart and soul,
waiting for your return.

~ quiet divine wisdom

*

What if this painful season
was always part of the plan?
What is it meant to reveal to you?
What blessing hides within?
Only you can uncover the truth.

~for you

*

Some fires burn briefly
and some continue to burn
for a long time.
Sometimes,
fires are purposely set
for various reasons.
Fires can be a reset,
no matter how devastating they are.
Allow yourself space
to rediscover your bearings.
Let the flames consume the bad
and leave you with nutritious soil
for renewal and growth
with supernatural grace.
Take this moment to sew
new seeds of beauty, love,
peace, and harmony.
Don't let the fire crush your soul—
but let it awaken your passion
to nurture new life with fervour again.

~purposeful planting

*

After enduring the fire,
few can truly relate.
Everyone has their own issues,
their own priorities.
Fires transform you,
leaving your skin raw,
your soul sensitive to heat.
Once burned,
you tread carefully
avoiding the flames again.
The memories remain
fixed and unforgotten.
Yet life gives you another chance
to embrace your purpose—
to be the artist of your existence.

~make it beautiful

*

No matter what has happened to you,
your future remains unwritten.
The past is only a memory
reminding you that darkness exists—
but so does beauty.
Your light holds the power to transform
even the darkest places
into something radiant.
Don't let the sun set
nor your story fade
before you grasp
the miracle of your existence—
the reason you survived it all.

~bring light to it all

*

Life isn't easy
and can change in a flash.
Yet the spirit within you
will guide you through this world
and beyond.
See life as a sacred passage—
a rite to arrive, express, and depart.
Choose love, faith, hope,
harmony, joy, passion,
and peace for all your days.
You will move with greater grace
when you let these virtues
guide your moments
and shape your life.

~guiding words

*

Fires burn hot, mesmerizing and powerful.
They warm us, feed us, protect us,
and light the way.
They deserve our reverence.
Still, fires can wound us deeply.
If we survive the flames,
we know we remain by grace.
There is a divine purpose
for our existence.
Our ultimate power lies
in choosing to align with love,
peace, and harmony—
to live this life as a miracle.

~the way

*

When you emerge from a fiery season,
you learn it can weaken you
or set your heart ablaze with passion—
sometimes both.
Allow yourself space to heal
in the way you need.
Wounds take time to repair,
even for the fastest healers.
Let your light return to its fullness,
and in due time,
you will shine so brightly,
the world will mistake you for the sun.
You were burning all along,
hidden beneath the ashes,
rising once more into the sky.

~rising

*

Fires are powerful forces.
They reshape and redefine
the existence of everything.
They create heat, organic matter, light,
warmth, and foster growth.
In many ways, the fires of life do the same.
They increase our potential,
providing kindling
for a life worth living.
Use the fire to become
the bonfire, the fireworks, the dynamite,
expressing all that stirs within your soul.
The brilliance of your light
can never be extinguished.

~light a fire

*

All fires must be respected—
hardships are the same.
When we honour the trials we've endured,
we come to see that every soul
has fought to stand here today.
Cheers to the lights
that shine even brighter,
for a past that demanded
they rise higher.

~one light to another

*

In time, you'll no longer hate the fire
that turned your world upside down.
You will come to see
it has equipped you
with supernatural power.
It transformed you— from victim to victor.
From helpless to powerful.
From uncertain to worthy.
You will learn that fires
transform you in ways
that only intense trials can.
Through the flames,
you are refined,
forged with the power
to turn challenges into triumphs.

~alchemist

*

Why did you need this fire in your life?
Fires, however devastating,
often serve a purpose.
This single question holds
a deluge of wisdom
to guide your journey ahead.

~take your power back

*

You will find that fires
burn through your fears
like nothing else can.
If you can endure the flames,
you can withstand anything.
This is the beauty of overcoming.

~force of nature

*

You will need time to integrate
what has happened.
The fire may be gone,
but its devastation does not vanish
nor does life magically resume.
It takes courage and presence
to sift through the remnants,
to mourn what was lost.
It also demands time, energy, and willpower
to rebuild, regrow,
and reimagine your life.
Be patient with yourself
in all the nuanced places you find yourself.

~it will come together

*

Every day will be different—
calling you to be present with yourself.
This is how you made it through,
and this is how you'll continue.
The fire revealed your strength;
and now it teaches you to use it.
As painful as it was,
it left you with remarkable gifts.
Allow them to guide you forward
through new challenges.
This is how warriors are shaped—
trained and entrusted with greater purpose.
You'll be given more
because you are capable of more.
This is the nature of life,
and you're stronger than you know.

~part of the training

*

Remember those moments
when you thought you couldn't go on—
and somehow you did?
Well, you made it.
And here you are, reading this.
Take a breath, a pause,
to honour all you've endured
and how you have emerged.
It was never in vain.
Only you need to acknowledge
what you survived,
what you overcame.
You and God are your witnesses.
Surrender to the moment
Allow yourself to be present—
with kindness, compassion, and love.
When you integrate your past,
you unlock the peace
to move forward with grace.
The fire taught you survival,
now let life teach you peace.

~the peace within

*

Pain may wound you deeply,
but it can never dim
the light within you.
Through the turmoil,
you discovered it did not break you—
it stripped away your weaknesses
and left behind resilience, determination,
compassion, kindness, and love.
You rose out of suffering,
by embracing your light,
not the darkness.

~holding the light

*

When you look back on all the memories,
you may still feel the fire.
It may make you weep,
a reminder of the value
they once held.
It's okay to feel—to let emotions rise
and remind you that you've survived.
Allow yourself to feel.
Each moment will be different,
offering something new.
When the time is right,
it will become your wisdom.

~be held in peace

*

After you've survived the fire,
You often take on its qualities.
At first, it was your teacher—
showing you how to endure
to rise above.
To survive, you became powerful,
you became fiery,
you became inexhaustible,
you became unstoppable,
and, most of all,
you became fearless.
These are the strengths you now hold,
greater than you ever imagined.
Use them wisely.
Shape them to serve your journey.

~the power you possess

*

After the flames around you
have finally settled,
you can start to listen
to the fire within.
Processing what happened
is no easy task—
give it time to be heard,
time to be nurtured.
Your energy is rising,
your heart ready to speak.
You're about to ignite your life
in the best and most powerful way.
This is your life, lived with purpose.
This is the gift of fire.

~your fire within

*

Fire has a way of creating chaos,
leaving you lost, unsure of where to turn.
It's the perfect storm—
tossing you about,
inflicting wounds,
frightening you to your core.
It will leave you exhausted and exasperated.
Yet, if you survive it,
you must find your bearings again,
reclaim who you are,
and rebuild the world around you.
With time and grace,
your compass will return.
So will your strength.
When love heals every part of you,
you'll learn that life is a gift—
and so was the fire.
It granted you the space to create anew,
with open eyes
and the wisdom of a beginner's mind.

~renewed

*

When you're in the fire,
the future disappears—
the present moment is all you have.
Survival consumes your every thought.
If you persevere,
you'll find a way break free—
wisdom will light your path.
Most fires in life
do not extinguish quickly,
no matter how much you wish
to put them out at once.
But fires temper you,
burning away impurities,
shaping something stronger.
So if you're here, reading this,
you are brave and resilient.
Your fire was your reset.
It took something so pain to reveal
that you're strong enough
to live life with courage
and an immense, unwavering grace.

~trial by fire

*

Let the fire you overcame
be your golden opportunity
to release the burdens, memories, and demands
that you carried into the flames.
They perished in the fire.
What you choose to take from it
is your strength.
You needed this fire for reasons
only your soul knows.
Give yourself time to uncover them.
This was the fire's lesson.
This was what your soul
needed you to understand
on your journey forward.

~the power to live

*

The thing about fire
is that when you're caught in one,
enduring pain is inevitable.
It does not discriminate—
it consumes everything.
Your fire could have taken anyone,
but it chose you.
There is no one to blame,
and even if there were,
blame is a losing battle.
Yet somehow, the fire has taught you
to take responsibility
for what remains—
no matter who ignited it.
In the end,
let the same divine love
that heals wounds on injured skin
also heal your heart, mind, spirit, and soul.

After you emerge,
your emotions may vacillate—
confusion, anger, unrest.

Let yourself feel the heaviness
without reaction.
After a while,
peace will find you again—
offering direction,
though you may fluctuate between states.
Be compassionate with yourself
as you return to your centre.
Let your emotions mature
as you steadily find your way.

~grow through it

*

Be patient with yourself.
After trauma,
it's natural to feel off-centre,
to be overcome with emotion.
As you heal, let divine love
enter places in your soul
that need mending,
that long to be restored.
Breath by breath,
it will grow easier.
And on the days it does not,
let the divine love circulate once more—
calming your soul,
returning you to peace.

~divine circulation

*

One day,
you will look back
and see how the fire transformed your life.
You will realize it ignited you
into a brighter force for this world.
Until then,
suspend all judgment.

~suspension

*

Life holds wonders for each of us.
Pain, the greatest teacher,
arrives with messages
only we can decode,
only we can receive.
Let's not give up until we uncover the gift
hidden within the fire.
Our mission is to emerge—
carrying these gifts within our souls,
as we step forward.
This is our divine purpose.

~the power to live

*

Not everyone will understand
what you've been through.
Your eyes will shine differently.
Take hold of inspiration,
and tend to the light within.
You don't have to carry the world.
When you save yourself,
your light will naturally
touch those around you.
Those ready to embrace your glow
will find you, and together,
the light will amplify.

~lighthouse

*

When you're pushed into a corner
with no way out in sight,
your divine intelligence
will carve a path for you.
And that's why you're here.
You surrendered to your light
and found your way through.
It's a miracle. You are a miracle.
The journey may have been painful,
but the harder the test,
the stronger you became.
You'll find that you can face anything.
This is your power now.
And it is yours to keep.

~it's yours

*

One day,
you'll see that the fire
gave you more than it took.
Keep going—
until that truth is revealed to you, my friend.

~enduring

*

The truth is, you have faced challenges—
they were hard,
but you overcame them.
Now, you know you can do hard things.
Let this be a reminder to your spirit,
whenever you need it.

~spirit of an overcomer

*

You will never forget your fires.
They carry the memories
of when your heart felt
branded by the flames.
Sometimes, your heart will sting
no matter how much time has passed.
That season transformed you,
ultimately emboldening you.
It revealed who you are
in the face of challenge—
and the ceaseless power
of your strength and love.

~relentless

*

Under pressure,
you discover the limits of your comfort zone.
But in fire,
you live far beyond them.
If beauty still finds you,
after the flames,
the fire has fulfilled its purpose.

~divine eyes

*

All fires
begin as small flames.
Something in your life
was calling for change,
but perhaps, at the time,
you couldn't see it.
So the fire grew
until it consumed you.
The truth is,
you needed the big fire.
You'll appreciate it
when you understand
what was hidden
within the smaller sparks.
This is your process of discovery.

~revelation

*

All the colours of a fire are beautiful,
but enduring one exposed you
to intensities that touched you
in unimaginable ways.
Some days, it felt unbearable.
Other moments, it left you numb.
By holding the conviction
that you would make it through,
an unstoppable divine power
moved through you
toward your most favourable outcome.

~destination destiny

*

You needed the fire to catapult your life.
And so it did.
Now, how do you want it to transform you?
That choice is entirely yours.

~driver's seat

*

Fires can feel like swimming in the ocean,
when we cannot swim.
They take on a life of their own—
calling forth the warrior within,
even when we want to return to shore.
In moments like these,
we must move with the current of wisdom,
while mustering the strength within us.
When the time is right,
we will break free, rise above,
and move beyond whatever has held us back.

~changing tide

*

There is a flame within you—
a light with the power to meet any fire
you face in life.
Don't be afraid of the flames.
Your light will find its way through.
A path will open—
a solution, a way, a miracle,
right when you need it most.
Expect to see what is meant for you—
your senses will guide you,
revealing what inspires where to gos
and what to do.
Face the fire.

~expect a path to open

*

When survival demands a fight for your life,
it unlocks an unfathomable strength.
How much will you endure?
The flames will reveal you your capacity,
your resolve to persevere.
Can you transform chaos into grace?
Hello, survivor,
you're doing just that.

~the grace to live

*

Fires can transform you
in brilliant ways.
Let them.
Let the fire consume everything
that isn't truly you
until they unveil—
your completeness,
your wholeness,
the truth,
the love.
When you rise from the ashes,
all that is divine will remain.
And yes, this is you.

~divinely you

*

Fill your heart with love,
and create your new life.
Let divine love guide you—
the light that carried you through your trials.
The meaning you assign to your survival
will shape your purpose ahead.
It's your secret sauce now,
the blaze that brings flavour
and colour to everything you do—
the magic you hold within.

~love sauce

*

Over time, things will inevitably settle.
and the fire you endured
will feel both surreal and strange.
But it did happen.
You did survive.
Those around you may not see it,
but deep in your soul,
you've been irrevocably changed.
Your triumph is forever yours—
etched in your eyes,
your heart,
and all you pour your energy into.
The world around you has shifted,
and you now face it
with a renewed warrior within.

~triumphant glow

*

It's okay if no one understands
the weight of what you've endured.
This journey belongs to your soul.
God knows exactly what it took
for you to stand here today.
You both know it wasn't easy.
And yet, here you are,
making sense of it all.
Let the pieces come together
when the time is right,
perfectly and naturally.
After all, puzzles only reveal their fullness
when you finish them.

~master pieces

*

This fire will forever hold
an intimate place in your heart.
It revealed your strength,
your courage,
your patience,
your persistence,
and your character.
Never diminish
the bravery it took
to reach this moment.

~the truth of your soul

*

Be kind to yourself
as you rebuild your life.
Starting from nothing
demands immense effort.
The fire taught you resilience under pressure,
and now it teaches you to rise with vigour
in all that you do.
Take the time you need
to focus your energy
on deliberate pursuits.
The fire rushed and pressured you,
but now is your time
to slow down and infuse purpose
into what gives fire to your soul.

~intentional steps

*

When your old self fades,
taking your former life,
you are rebirthed anew.
Your new existence calls you
to live with courage, love, and beauty.
It urges you to let go
of everything else.
You cannot return
to the way things were—
that path has vanished.
Clean and naked,
this journey asks you
to walk with love in your heart—
the force that saved you.
Can you summon courage once more?
Your new self beckons you
to recommit to your life—
and rediscover its beauty.

~new committment

*

Some days, the fire will feel
as vivid as yesterday;
other days, it won't occupy
all your daily thoughts.
When fire touches your heart,
you carry it forever—
the pain that tore it apart,
and the power it sparked
in the very same breath.
This is the place
of your death and rebirth.

~transformation

*

When you escape a fire,
you'll spend time checking
to ensure that it's safe.
Everything may still feel hot,
and as life moves forward,
it's okay to be cooling off,
letting the heat on your skin fade.
When will it stop feeling tender?
When will you speak of the fire,
without emotion
or sensing it in your body?
Give yourself the grace to feel it all.
Your experience matters—
it's valid and important.
Allow yourself to heal in the way
that restores your soul.

~divine healing

*

The fire brought you back to life,
rekindling something within
that was waiting to be born.
It took a deep pain
to bring you to the surface.
Do not grieve what happened,
for life is calling you forward.
As with all pain,
goodness often follows
in overwhelming waves.
So hold on, and be ready for the good
that will come from all of this.
The tides are turning,
and your moment is near.

~the life that's calling you

*

Fires refine,
and that's what they did to you.
They burned away the things
most dear to your heart.
Yet, those treasures,
etched deeply in your soul,
will always remain.
Within you,
their love endures,
living on forever.

~the sacred place

*

Use the energy of the fire to inspire you.
You were given a reset—
a chance to begin anew.
Recreate yourself.
What excites you?
What ignites your passion?
What fills you with joy?
What lifts you higher?
There's no set timeline
for when you'll feel ready to explore;
you'll know.
This is the beginning of you,
authentically present
in this moment.
In time, you'll see that the fire
was no accident.
It burned to ignite your light
so that you could illuminate the world.
For now,
nurture the fire rising in you.

~tend to your fire

*

It's okay
to seek solitude
to retreat to your cave
after walking through the fire.
Fires are intense.
To find balance again,
you'll need calmness, solace, and stillness.
Healing often flows from opposing energies,
restoring equilibrium and integrity
where it's most needed.
For a while, you may crave peace—
until you steady yourself once more.
This is okay,
it's natural,
it's essential.
Embrace this time
as you rediscover yourself.
And when the moment feels right,
don't forget to return
to the world outside.

~cave time

*

A fire teaches wisdom
like nothing else can.
It touches every part of your mind,
body, heart, spirit, and soul—
no part of you is off-limits.
Each colour melts a different part of you.
In the deepest cleansing of your life,
you emerge with more wisdom
inspirited into the fabric of who you are.
As you return to the world,
you carry the essence
of your purest, highest self.

~deep clean

*

Navigating your hardships,
you must hold the light within—
without it, you risk losing your way.
Stay faithful to the light within you,
you'll find that your hardships
are not your enemies.
They lift your spirit
beyond your obstacles.
When you centre yourself
in your divine power,
you'll realize that nothing can destroy you.
The hardships and the darkness
will fade away,
as long as you hold faithfully
to your inner light.

~be faithful to the light

*

Fires change you—
They strip away everything,
leaving you bare.
But, as you recover,
you'll find a deeper truth:
your spiritual wealth has grown
in ways that nothing can ever take away.

~inner growth

*

Being on fire
Left you feeling alone and lost.
Rising from the flames,
you'll feel disoriented at first.
But with time,
you'll rediscover your direction,
your purpose—
the life within you.
Allow yourself the space and time,
to feel it all:
every wave, every emotion,
every dip, every tear.
You aren't alone.
You're held by the One
who has been with you all along—
your saving grace.

~never alone

*

All emotions are valid.
You'll experience so much
at every moment of the day.
Your body will seek to process it all.
While your mind tries to make sense of it.
Let your body breathe
through the challenging moments.
Stay present and steady.
Show your emotions that they're safe—
safe to emerge, to release,
to be held in the fullness of your being.
Through this flow of energy,
the triggers will be felt,
the pain will move through you.
And, as if by a miracle,
peace will find you again.
Be present with loving kindness,
present for each sensation,
then, mindfully, let it all go.

~held in peace

*

We all face our fires—
burning with an intensity
that sears us to our core.
When engulfed by the flames,
our divine strength within
becomes our sole reliance.
Our soul whispers:
do not give up.
Your mission here is not complete.
So we persist,
praying for divine peace
to carry us through.
The path out of darkness,
is found in holding our light,
steadfast in every moment.

~your light is your strength

*

This fire stripped you bare,
leaving only your soul exposed.
From this place, you begin anew.
You're left with everything you need—
the gifts you carried into this world:
love, wholeness,
unity, value,
and harmony.
From this foundation,
you'll rebuild your home again.

~home of love

*

All this talk of fire
can leave you feeling burned,
sad, and weepy.
It reflects every emotion you've endured.
It's never easy
to have nowhere to return to,
while managing challenge and discomfort.
This is where a part of you died—
but also where you were reborn,
with a will to survive,
and the power to know
that you can ignite a new life.

~infinite spirit

*

Don't give up.
God could already have taken you,
but your purpose was to remain.
Pause, breathe, and stand still.
The power that saved you
will empower you
to thrive in whatever comes next.
This inner power—
always alive and moving within you—
persists, even when you forget.
Move forward,
knowing you have the strength you need.

~breath of life

*

You don't need to linger
around the remains of the fire;
you've already endured it.
You've been given the knowledge to escape—
that is your truth now.
Share what you know,
and let healing find you.
Healing happens in the space you allow—
space to soothe your spirit,
to rediscover what goodness feels like,
and to rest in the comfort
of your being.
Let yourself be.
Let yourself move toward what grounds you.
In the beginning, it will feel unsteady—
perhaps for a while.
But with intention and patience,
chaos will yield to order
Give yourself love and nurturance.
And above all,
extend compassion to yourself
as you navigate new terrain.

~space to be

*

When you're delievered from fire,
you don't know how it feels
to live outside its flames.
You've been running for so long—
trying to survive,
shielding yourself,
searching for air.
It'll take time to trust
that it's safe to exhale,
and that not everything
will be taken from you.
Life will come back,
and you must hold onto the truth:
what is unburnable remains within you.
It is enduring, intact,
unstoppable, and ever-present.

~with you always

*

Everyone faces a different season:
one person emerges from the fire,
one resides within it,
one walks toward a wildfire,
one finds joy beside a campfire,
one celebrates with a bonfire,
one marvels at fireworks,
one narrowly escapes an explosion.
Fires come in all forms,
but none lack power.
There's a purpose within every blaze,
even when it defies our understanding.
By allowing our divine intelligence
to unravel its meaning,
we rise victorious.

~fire season

*

You'll uncover the gift of everything
when you're pushed
beyond your limits.
You'll remember all that nourishes your soul—
the people who matter deeply,
the small moments that brought you relief,
the comforts that renewed your spirit,
the soft places that echo grace.
As you rebuild yourself,
these gifts become essential,
granting you the strength
to dream once more.

~returning home

*

You'll search for signs of smoke—
staying vigilant of what causes fire,
what can ignite,
what smells of fire,
and what looks like flames.
This is your body and mind on high alert for pain.
It'll take space and distance
for your nervous system to ease—
to stop reacting to everything.
This is normal.
You are normal.
Allow yourself to observe your behaviours,
without judgement.
The fire gave you wisdom,
teaching you to grasp its power.
It's not your enemy.
It reveals a part of you
that holds the same power—
to bring life and death to all it touches.
If you're here,
the fire is reminding you
to rise with life.

~always choose life

*

When something transforms you
so profoundly and painfully,
you'll discover a new version of yourself.
One who is softer,
yearning for peace, love, and harmony.
This shift is natural
when nothing is the same anymore.
You've stepped off the fight-flight-freeze ride,
and your nervous system
longs for calm over stimulation.
Grant yourself the space
to decompress and relax.
Your divine spirit will guide you,
showing you the moment
to channel your power into your purpose.

~divine timing

*

There's no set timeline,
no measuring stick to tell you
when you'll reconnect with your true self.
Trauma is disorienting,
so give yourself patience and compassion.
Restoration will happen
as you rebuild your inner world
with your highest virtues—
the qualities that carried you through
life's most challenging trials:
love, truth,
perseverance, faith,
and wisdom.
Let these divine qualities guide you
as you find your way
back to yourself.

~you have what you need

*

People around you
may not grasp
what you've been through—
and that's okay.
You're the one tasked with processing it all
and uncovering its meaning.
Seek those who offer support
free of judgement and pressure.
You've reached the other side,
but that doesn't mean it was easy
or that your battles are behind you.
You had to lose parts of your life
to arrive where you are now.
And from this humble place,
you'll learn to live again—
to plant new roots
and begin anew.

~rising up

*

You'll undergo profound spiritual shifts,
transformations that touch
your mind, heart, and soul.
For a time, you may feel like an outsider—
though it might have little to do with others.
You'll crave peace
and the need to reconnect inwardly.
The fire awakened this in you.
It was the only place the fire couldn't harm you.
Now, you'll feel drawn to
understanding your spirit, growing with it,
and letting it guide you.
From here, you'll learn
to navigate a physical world—
a world that's burnable,
temporary, fickle, and often untrustworthy.
Your soul wants connection with what remains
untouched by death—
the ceaseless, the permanent, the truthful.
Here lies the wisdom and love
that empower you to live
humbly and gratefully
for all that is eternal and true.

~divine connection

*

Stillness and quiet
will soothe your soul—
let them.
Listen, meditate,
converse with your soul.
Commune with your Creator.
You'll find your feet again,
and in time, you'll rekindle your fire
to burn brightly for life once more.
Be gentle with yourself,
as you decide where to move
and how to direct your energy.
You were guided out of the fire,
and you'll continue to be led
in the best possible way.
Your mission isn't over,
dear friend.

~fueled by fire

*

There's no right way to heal;
it's a process of returning to yourself,
of learning to reignite your fire
each time it runs low.
Stay open to sparks of inspiration—
they'll carry you through moments
and stretches of pain.
As you confront yourself,
bit by bit,
you'll feel your wheels turning once more.

~move with inspiration

*

Throughout history,
revival has followed survival.
Be patient in the moments
when you feel you can't go on—
a sign, synchronicity, or inspiration
will show you're on the right path.
Be mindful of what's being revealed.
You were made for more,
and it had to be burned out of you.
When one thing ends,
another is naturally born.
It's the law of order.
You're emerging from your season of strife
and stepping into your season of greatness.
Embrace it fully.

~revival time

*

Life reveals its greatest gift
when you feel you have nothing left.
When your spirit has been through the ringer,
and you're overwhelmed with emotion,
grace will find you again.
What holds you together,
is the thing that will keep you moving forward.
Even if it feels like you're held together
by the thinnest thread—
that thread is your divine soul:
the strength instilled in you by the Creator,
a force that outlasts and outlives
every situation and circumstance.
You were made to endure.
The divine carefully wove you together
with the spirit of a survivor.

~weaved in gold

*

The world around you has changed.
It will continue to shift,
and for a while,
life will feel different.
You'll question everything,
missing pieces of your old life.
Everyone around you
is navigating their own path,
and so are you.
Your energy will be drawn to places
that allows it to heal.
Be healed.
Be held.
Be nurtured.
Let yourself feel safe again.
Reconnect with your wholeness.

~embracing it all

*

It takes courage to stand here—
to face the unknown
and create meaning in a finite world.
Whatever unifies your heart, mind, spirit, and soul—
is your calling.
When you live in harmony with your true self,
you'll flow through life,
and everything will align.
A supernatural force
Is always supporting you.
When you listen and act with wisdom,
life becomes easier.
If your heart, mind, and spirit feel misaligned,
seek to uncover what's disrupting your flow.
This is your chance to reconnect
with your divine essence—
loving, faith-filled, and serene.
Keep moving forward.
Your breakthrough is near.

~supernatural guidance

*

The fire will change you profoundly—
more than anything in your life.
Though everything feels unsteady now,
one day you'll reflect
and realize the fire was forging
a season of your finest work,
your greatest mission,
your deepest personal growth.
In time, you'll understand.

~in the making

*

Everything is tied together
in the spiritual realm.
There are no coincidences—
it all unfolded as needed,
guiding you toward the path
you were meant to take.
Your soul had to endure,
to reach a higher plane,
because the road you once travelled
could never have allowed you
to swim, soar, and love
as you do now.

~loving more

*

On your most challenging days,
remember the fire—
what it awakened within you.
That power is yours,
unchanged and enduring.
It makes you unstoppable,
even when you feel uncertain,
when fear rises,
and the burns still linger.
Now, it's a different setting,
but the same knowledge and wisdom
will lift you above whatever stands before you.
You will rise. You will succeed.
That is certain.

~everything you are

*

As a survivor of the fire,
you've learned you can outlast
the most tragic, harrowing trials
known to humanity.
This is no small feat.
On the days you doubt your strength,
anchor yourself in the truth of who you are.
Someone else in your exact position,
might not have withstood what you did.
For a divine reason,
you're still here.
Nothing happens by chance.
You are meant to be here—
to ignite your purpose
and set it ablaze.
Do what calls to your soul:
the things you couldn't do before,
the things you wanted to do,
the things the world needs from you,
and the things you need from yourself.
This is why you're here.
This next season belongs to you.

~your season

*

Life's hardships reveal truths.
They show us that:
love has the power to heal,
kindness has the strength to uplift,
care is born from the heart,
peace carries a divine essence,
and integrity is a guiding light.
These are the reasons to live—
because nothing else matters.
This world needs your love, life, and light.
Your purpose remains, unwavering.
Through love, kindness, care,
peace, and integrity,
you'll create and rebuild a life
shaped by these virtues.
These are the qualities of a healed world.

~living with grace

*

As we pick up the pieces of our lives,
we'll find there is no energy left
to cast blame.
We know tragedy steals time too,
and we refuse to lose any more of it.
We know that life is now
it is here,
and someday,
it will vanish once more.
Through tragedy,
we are given the chance to glimpse death,
before it arrives,
granting us the opportunity
to resurrect our lives
in ways that only love can.
And so, with love,
we move forward.

~guided by love

*

It's okay to move slow some days—
let the sun rise over the city,
kiss your face,
set beyond the hill,
and still find yourself in the same place.
These slower days, the ones you've longed for,
are an invitation to simply be.
Be present.
Let the beauty surrounding you
come into focus.
If you look for it,
it's all you can see.

~the peace of stillness

*

This fire was a reset.
healing and mending your heart
will take some time.
But one day,
you'll accept that it happened—
and it won't burn you
that it did.
Love alone has the power to do this for you.

~love is your healer

*

When trials test the core of your being,
you begin to grasp
the truths of light and dark.
Every day brings a battle
light against darkness—
and when caught in the fire,
you must choose quickly
which side you're on.
You're now awakened to your spiritual path,
learning to discern what's bright and life-giving
and what is bright yet destructive.

~discernment

*

Hardships
come in countless forms.
But it's the ones that demand endurance,
and make you face your own humanity—
the brush of death,
that show you how much you want to live.
Your purpose remains unfulfilled
here on planet Earth.
Life needs your light
and patiently waits for you.
What was it that called you back to life?

~your flame of purpose

*

When pain confronted you
from every direction,
you created a path
within yourself
to light the way forward.
That same power
will guide you
through every season in your life.
It's the truest, clearest,
purest, most loving
expression of who you are.
Surrender to your divine essence
and let it light the way
to your promised land.

~light leads to freedom

*

Acceptance is the bridge to our destiny.
It's embracing the past for what it was
and drawing lessons from it.
It's understanding what we couldn't before,
and turning it into strength to move forward.
Through understanding the truth,
we learn how to live more wisely
Without understanding,
we're more likely to fall into the same traps.
Transforming our pain through correction
is the key to our freedom.

~the power of understanding

*

When we find ourselves in a challenging trial,
we face aspects of life
beyond our control—
frightening, disheartening,
and heavy with anxiety.
In these moments,
we learn that intentional actions
can sustain us.
These strategies, once embraced,
become tools for future challenges.
Return to love,
anchor ourselves in peace.
Choose life.
Take small steps forward.
Be present.
Extend kindness to ourselves and others.
Rest in the divine strength within us.

~harmonize your being

*

Reflecting on our harrowing experience,
we'll find that love was the force
that carried us through.
The unconditional love within us,
and the love from those who reminded us
that we were never alone.
They may not have understood
the depth of our pain,
but their empathy
became our strength.
This is the medicine we all need—
the purity, healing, and wholeness
that only love and empathy can bring.

~healing medicine

*

Everyone's story of their fire
is uniquely different.
Each of us must pick up the pieces
of a life transformed
and create a new one.
It's vital to return
to the essence of who we are—
the love, the peace,
the wholeness, the faith,
and strength.
From this foundation,
we can rebuild,
guided by divine wisdom
that empowers us to live
from our brightest light.
Ultimately, this path leads to life.

~choose life

*

Life-changing events
can happen to anyone,
but this one happened to you.
It's your overcomer's spirit
that has brought you here.
Your light is meant to guide others,
to show them they too can triumph
over their battles.
Now that you're here,
what fuels your light to shine even brighter?
Let your spirit reveal your answer.

~a beacon of light

*

The hardships you've endured
almost extinguished your spirit,
Yet they ignited your greatness.
This strength has always resided within you,
and now you understand the truth—
you can break free from limitations.
Everything you've overcome
testifies to your divine power,
a resilience that conquers darkness.
In times of struggle,
lean into this divine wisdom;
it grants you the grace to know
you can withstand every battle you face.
With humility and gratitude,
you'll come to recognize
this tremendous gift you've received.
You possess the power to triumph
over all darkness,
fueled by the light
that glows within you.

~superpower

*

With newfound understanding
and a renewed approach to fighting darkness,
new possibilities have come to life.
The fire has awakened your consciousness
to a greater you,
capable of anything.
Use this life
to fulfill what you've always dreamed of:
to breathe possibility into your vision;.
to colour new places;
to tread new paths;
to bring meaning to life;
to know yourself more deeply;
to find your spiritual wings.
What calls to your spirit?
What purpose remains for you to embrace?

~it's all within you

THANK YOU FOR PURCHASING RISING FROM THE FIRE

Thank you very much for purchasing my book. I hope this book not only uplifts but also inspires and transforms your heart, mind, spirit, and soul, empowering your journey with a new perspective. The right words can give you a new energy to light your way.

If you've found Rising From the Fire to be a source of inspiration and value, please share your thoughts in a review. Your feedback is not just appreciated; it's invaluable. It will help other readers find this book and spread the love. Thank you once again!

Warmly,

Muriel Okubo

SUBSCRIBE TO MY NEWSLETTER

Find me on my website: okubowellness.com
Follow me on IG: @muriel.okubo @okubowellness

ABOUT THE AUTHOR

Muriel Okubo is a Canadian-Japanese author, artist, and Doctor of Traditional Asian Medicine. She has had a busy practice for over sixteen years in which she has treated people from all walks of life and all ages struggling with various issues. Having witnessed the pains of the human condition and the beauty of the human spirit, she wishes to inspire and encourage everyone on their path.

Understanding that body-mind-spirit health is crucial for wellness, she has created beautiful books to help people integrate their physical, mental, emotional, and spiritual bodies. She has always loved the power of writing as a connection to her heart and soul. Muriel is passionate about sharing the ideas and practices that have helped her the most on her path to living more consciously. She desires that everyone follow their inner wisdom and find the truth of their soul.

www.ingramcontent.com/pod-product-compliance
Lightning Source LLC
Chambersburg PA
CBHW021337140626
46545CB00020B/2367

* 9 7 8 1 9 9 8 6 9 5 0 5 8 *